Jihad
Myth & Reality

Brigadier (R)
Najeeb Ullah Khan

CreativePublishing

Creative Publishing
59 – Usman block
New Garden Town
Lahore, Pakistan
T: +92 42 35855344-6
+92 42 35844345-6

First published in Pakistan.
This edition 2013

ISBN 978 969 9932 00 7

Printed and bound in Pakistan by
Creative Publishing

Dedicated to
my wife and daughters

A Word from the Writer and
Foreword by the first reader

1.   I am not a religious scholar and, indeed, not a scholar at all. However I have been interested to know more and more about our Faith. My private diary which I started writing 10th December 1973, has a hint to this effect. So I would have been pondering over this even earlier and, of course, later as well. Despite very heavy professional commitments till retirement on 20th April 1995 (having passed out 19th April, 34 years earlier) I continued to try to spend the available time to read Qur'an. May Allah, the Beneficent, the Merciful forgive me – it was never simple recitation but always with translation and, at times, only translation. Starting with Tafheem-Ul-Qur'an (6 volumes), through Maarif-Ul-Qur'an (8 volumes), onto English translation by Pickthall and Abdullah Yousaf Ali's English translation with explanatory notes and comments (dictionary terms it exegesis, for Bible). One or two other urdu 'tafaseer' were also at hand with a couple of later times English translations. Out of these, Tarjiman-Ul-Quran by Maulana Abul Kalam Azad also proved useful. May Allah Bless souls of all of them for the phenomenal effort for their works, Amen. Other than the above, I would have been reading religion oriented material appearing in the newspapers I got (different at different times). Let me admit the faith came to me in a hard way. But I consider myself fortunate that, although coming slowly and not easily yet, it appears to be growing on firm roots! May God that I am progressing on right lines, Amen. For otherwise I will be in a precarious position having prayed (1992, for the first time) that He may lift

me up when He thinks I would not go any higher spiritually.

2.   As per my diary of the study of Qur'an, 1st October 2011 (my 72nd birthday) I had completed reading of the Qur'an for the third time – this last being a deeper study stretching over three years starting 5 July 2008. Allow me to interject with a remark I made at a few occasions as I progressed on my understanding of the Qur'an and noticing new vistas – "There is no final reading of the Qur'an" (jotted down on the sacred pages; as also other observations with dates forming like a diary). At this stage I decided to study the Qur'an topic wise and, without much thought, decided on 'Jihad'. As said earlier, my general reading had been very limited – mostly to the newspapers. I had never written anything considered worth publishing except one article that I offered for publication in the GHQ Journal. It was on the topic of 'Internal Security' based on my experience as an operations staff officer in a Division deployed on this duty in Baluchistan. Its publication was declined for 'security' reasons. However, a few years later, and after some editing, I had it published in the college magazine of Military College of Engineering Risalpur (now part of NUST) where I was the Commandant! I am stating all this only to highlight my deficiency despite which I decided to undertake this effort. But I have tried to do it with maximum diligence I could muster, and sense of responsibility, going over the relevant material threadbare taking more than a year and a half.

English translation of the sacred verses has been taken from Pickthall's The Glorious Quran.

3.   The first person to read this study was General Ayaz Ahmad who commented on telephone: "A very good effort in, surprisingly, good English. A nice 'cut and dry' style – to the point". Please treat this as 'Foreword' from him, meaning he never knew me as a writer, even less as a scholar.

Introduction

1. There are a number of misconceptions about Islam in the minds of its non-adherents. The most sensitive, a current misunderstanding springs from the propaganda that Islam is another name for terrorism, which allegedly, permits religious violence and coercive conversion under the threat of naked sword, all in the name of the Jihad. This study is going to be an informed discourse to prove that the above assertion is not true; indeed such misunderstandings appear to spring from the historical perspective of armed clashes between the Islamic and the Christian worlds for more than a thousand years. During the first half of this period Islam, emerging initially out of the Arabian Peninsula, quickly spread itself far and wide conquering territories including that of its First 'Kaaba' and parts of South Eastern Europe. This situation was challenged in the Middle Ages by the Christian world of Europe who tried to reclaim their Holy Land by fighting the famous battles termed Crusades. This clash of ideologies and cultures continued for the next half a millennium during the later part of which Islam was no more the dominant religion. It is this constant religio-cutlural clash that has dominated the thinking of the Western writers and researchers, which further influenced the public opinion, while all kinds of vested interests played their usual part to reinforce propaganda that Islam believes in perpetual religious violence and proselytizing

through coercion. Let me here quote what Sir Thomas Arnold, a Western scholar and a prominent orientalist, has to say on this subject:

"There are no passages to be found in the Qur'an that in any way enjoin forcible conversion, and many that on the contrary, limit propagandist efforts to preaching and persuasion." He further adds "no passage in the Qur'an authorizes unprovoked attacks on unbelievers and that in accordance with such teaching, all the wars of Muhammad were defensive."

(The Preaching of Islam 4th Edition 1979, p-451 as quoted in 'Renaissance' June 2002, p-72).

2. On the other side of the spectrum is Sir William Muir who, commenting on Surah Al Tauba, has been quoted as saying:

"Sir William Muir, while relating the publication of some verses of the ninth chapter of the Koran on the occasion of the great pilgrimage A.H. 9, and referring to the opening verses of the Sura (from 1st to 7th inclusive) writes: "The Pilgrimage just quoted completed the system of Mahomet so far as its relations with idolatrous tribes and races were concerned. The few cases of truce excepted, uncompromising warfare was declared against them all."

(Paragraph 40 of the Book 'Critical Exposition of the Popular Jihad' by Maulvi (or Maulana) Chiragh Ali)

The above divergence of views between two 'knighted' English scholars shows that an objective study on the subject of Jihad is not going to be easy. The way forward would be to consciously cast aside all prejudices and preconceived ideas and proceed with an open mind to study injunctions of the Quran along with the lifetime practices of the Prophet of Islam on how these injunctions and edicts were followed in letter and spirit. It is all the more important in view of the fact that there has existed a schism even amongst the Muslims; and the unique concept of Jihad – a vital pillar of the Islamic faith - has not always been appreciated in its right spirit. There had been internecine battles among the Muslim groups right in the early Islamic era while an internal political strife is known to have continued all these centuries within the Muslim 'fraternity'. With this brief background, we may now proceed with our study of the topic of Jihad, which has been subjected to severe criticism by people of other faiths.

3.   Please note Jihad and Qital are usually considered synonymous but, in fact, the former is a vaster term and includes the latter which is fighting in the field

if peaceful means fail to enforce the order Allah ordains for a human society. With the help of the Trilingual Subject Index of the Qur'an prepared by 'Islamic Research Foundation' (Pages 642 to 670) I was able to locate nearly one hundred and fifty (150) verses relating to Jihad (including Qital). Nearly half of these are in the form of exhortation to strive or fight in the way of Allah while others ordain specific injunctions related to different situations and groups of people; and, interestingly, many verses are like principles of war as taught in the modern military codes. I have tried to concern myself mainly with the verses more directly related to Jihad (or Qital). It is important to understand that Jihad and faith are intertwined. Bedrock of Jihad is the faith that God has selected Al-Islam as our religion and it has to prevail over all other religions. Also granting of faith, which is the most precious blessing of God, is solely His Prerogative. This and one or two other facets of faith thus form part of our discussion.

4. Treating it as an informed discourse, I have freely given my views and comments all along. I request the reader to minutely look through all the explanatory notes given at the start of a Surah, a verse or a group of verses, and also at the end of the quoted verses (specifically paras 30 to 32) to facilitate quicker comprehension. Let me add here that the real crunch comes on reaching Surah Al-

Tauba (revealed 9H) much criticized by the non-muslim scholars for the stern commandments there in particular the Jizya clause (Verse 29). Background to the stern edicts, so to say, has been covered at paras 16 to 19 with additional comment in para 20, and Jizya clause at paras 21 to 23, all proving that these commandments in their real import are not so stern as they appear on cursory reading (indeed para 16 to 22 will read like a brief treatise on the subject). Outline of remaining discourse is give below:

- Para 23 briefly summarizes the Qur'anic injunctions up to this point (para 22).

- Paras 24 - 25 and paras 33 – 34 elaborate on how the misguided and basically ignorant individuals and groups can be exploited in the name of Jihad.

- Paras 26 – 27 cover the fact that the Prophet did not initiate hostilities in any of the battles he fought. However, he did not forgive treachery or repeated breaking of pledges / treaties. In case of threat of imminent enemy action he resorted to pre-emptive strikes. Only in case of Khaebar the detractors do not accept this but that is without good reason.

- Para 28: Hallmark in all actions of the Prophet was his resolve to ensure peaceful environment for his preaching mission. There was not a single case of forced conversion as he was only a messenger to convey the divine message and had not been sent as a warder or a keeper over them.

- Para 29: Faith is the greatest blessing of God. Para 29 onward cover some interesting facets of the subject of faith.

- Para 30: Will all born Muslims by sheer that stroke of luck ultimately go to paradise while the non-muslims are foredoomed to go to Hell!

- Para 31: The Qur'an throws an open challenge to all mankind (Jinn as well if we could locate them) to get together and produce a few Surahs or even a few verses like those in Qur'an. The Prophet of Al-Islam, unlike other honored prophets did not show any miracles in the traditional sense. But Qur'an is a constant miracle.

- Para 32: Not many prophets met with much worldly success in their lifetimes. Should we then feel too small to strive for Islam to prevail over all other religions? What can we do to be included in the category to be Blessed by God?

- Para 33: Jihad of Afghanistan

- Para 34: Jihad by the TPP

- Para 35: Granting faith is God's Prerogative. What is our responsibility and duty? Those who don't ponder and don't pay heed are worse than cattle.

5. Let us now move on to the sacred text of the verses covering the above broad perspective of our study.

Surah Al-Hajj (22)

Verse 39 is the first verse revealed on the subject of Jihad or Qital. In this and the following two verses, followers of the Prophet, who had been forced to emigrate from Mecca due to unabated persecution in all forms including inhuman physical torture, are being allowed to fight.

V - 39
"Sanction is given unto those who fight because they have been wronged; and Allah is indeed Able to give them victory."
V – 40
(First part) – "Those who have been driven from their homes unjustly only because they said: Our Lord is Allah - "

(Second part – giving-God's other reason for granting sanction to fight back) – "For had it not been for Allah's repelling some men by means of others, cloisters and churches and oratories and mosques, wherein the name of Allah is oft mentioned, would assuredly have been pulled down. Verily Allah helpeth one who helpeth Him. Lo! Allah is Strong, Almighty –"

Having been given hope for victory (V – 39 above) God expects that the Muslims shall establish His Order enunciated in the next verse:

14

V – 41

"Those who, if We give them power in the land, establish worship and pay the poor-due and enjoin kindness and forbid iniquity. And Allah's is the sequel of events."

6. Verses 58 and 60 mention the excesses committed against people forcing them to flee from their homes, but then advising them against excess in revenge:

V – 58

"Those who fled their homes for the cause of Allah and then were slain or died, Allah verily will provide for them a good provision. Lo! Allah, He verily is Best of all who make provision."

V – 60

"That (is so). And whoso hath retaliated with the like of that which he was made to suffer and then hath (again) been wronged, Allah will succour him. Lo! Allah verily is Mild, Forgiving."

(Also see Verse 194 of Surah Al-Baqarah)

7. Verse 78 is comprehensive enough covering faith, quality of our effort in its support, naming us Muslims from the start and now, the Messenger being witness against us, and we as witnesses against mankind – a very great status which we

shall be expected to justify through the indicated practical actions.

V – 78
"And strive for Allah with the endeavour which is His right. He hath chosen you and hath not laid upon you in religion any hardship; the faith of your father Abraham (is yours). He hath named you Muslims of old time and in this (Scripture), that the messenger may be a witness against you, and that ye may be witnesses against mankind. So establish worship, pay the poor-due, and hold fast to Allah. He is your Protecting friend. A blessed Patron and a blessed Helper!"

Surah Al-Baqarah (2)

8. In the verses 190 onwards Muslims are ordained to fight against all kinds of persecution and injustice (termed to "fight in the way of Allah"), but then imposing conditions worth serious note:

One – Don't initiate hostilities, i.e. don't commit aggression

Two – And hold back if the enemy desists, i.e. don't transgress

Three – Don't fight in the Inviolable Place of Worship and during the declared sacred months.

But if they violate the sacred prohibition, then you may go all out (slay them to teach them a lesson);

Four – Attack in the like manner and don't exceed in revenge i.e. don't fight relentlessly. However persecution, which has been termed worse than slaughter, must be eliminated. And this, perhaps, is the sum and substance of the term Jihad (repeated almost in identical words in verse 193 here and verse 39 of Surah Al-Anfal) implying that religious freedom and civil rights should not be denied on the basis of faith.

Finally you are expected to spend all your resources to thwart aggression.

V – 190
"Fight in the way of Allah against those who fight against you, but begin not hostilities. Lo! Allah loveth not aggressors."

V – 191
"And slay them wherever ye find them, and drive them out of the places whence they drove you out, for persecution is worse than slaughter. And fight not with them at the Inviolable Place of Worship until they first attack you there, but if they attack you (there) then slay them. Such is the reward of disbelievers."

V – 192

"But if they desist, then lo! Allah is Forgiving, Merciful."

V – 193

"And fight them until persecution is no more, and religion is for Allah. But if they desist, then let there be no hostility except against wrong-doers."

V – 194

"The forbidden month for the forbidden month, and forbidden things in retaliation. And one who attacketh you, attack him in like manner as he attacked you. Observe your duty to Allah, and know that Allah is with those who ward off (evil)."

Earlier on, this injunction appeared in V 60 (Al-Hajj).

V – 195

"Spend your wealth for the cause of Allah, and be not cast by your own hands to ruin; and do good. Lo! Allah loveth the beneficent."

9. Verse 217 is in the backdrop of a Muslim troop taking aggressive action against enemy during a sacred month, which was without approval and subsequently openly reproved by the Prophet. The verse also touches upon the subject of renegades, which shall appear in greater detail under Surah

'Ale `Imran.

V – 217

"They question thee (O Muhammad) with regard to warfare in the sacred month. Say: Warfare therein is a great (transgression), but to turn (men) from the way of Allah, and to disbelieve in Him and in the Inviolable Place of Worship, and to expel His people thence, is a greater (transgression) with Allah; for persecution is worse than killing. And they will not cease from fighting against you till they have made you renegades from your religion, if they can. And whoso becometh a renegade and dieth in his disbelief: such are they whose works have fallen both in the world and the Hereafter. Such are rightful owners of the Fire: they will abide therein."

10. Verses 216, 218 & 244 are mainly a kind of exhortation to fight in the way of Allah.

V – 216

"Warfare is ordained for you, though it is hateful unto you; but it may happen that ye hate a thing which is good for you, and it may happen that ye love a thing which is bad for you. Allah knoweth, ye know not."

V – 218

"Lo! those who believe, and those who emigrate (to

escape the persecution) and strive in the way of Allah, these have hope of Allah's mercy. Allah is Forgiving, Merciful."

V – 244
"Fight in the way of Allah, and know that Allah is Hearer, Knower."

Surah Al-'Anfal (8)

11. Most part of this Surah was revealed in the year 2H in the aftermath of the Signal Muslim victory at Badr. A lot of war booti (spoils of war) fell at their hands which included many prisoners of war passed on as captives or slaves to the Muslim fighters. Some of the important elements relating to the subject of our study are detailed below followed by the sacred text of the relevant verses:-

a. Exhortation to the Muslims to be ready to fight on if persecution of the believers is not stopped; however, past can be forgiven.

b. Half hearted Muslims (later termed hypocrites) are being warned that there shall be no compromise in the matter of faith in Al-Islam.

c. A stricter edict is against those who keep changing their loyalties and break treaties at will. They, along with their supporters, are to be treated with an iron hand after "throwing back" their treaties.

d.   Peace overtures should be favorably responded.

e.   Notwithstanding a decisive victory at Badr an important failing has been highlighted namely - the enemy fighters should have been the first and the main target and not any kind of booti. Indeed this forms an important principle of war even in the modern warfare for the reason that once the enemy fighting force is crushed the field will be yours. This lesson was again ignored by a section of the Muslim force in the next major battle of Uhad at a perilous cost.

f.   Make all preparations for war to be able to talk from a position of strength.

g.   Strength of the enemy was observed to be considerably more than the Prophet saw in his dream and as an eye illusion before the battle. So he fervently prayed and pleaded for Divine help. Allah indicated help by one thousand angels (and what could they not achieve?) But then it was only as "good tidings" and "reassurance" to raise morale of the Muslim fighters. Let me here quote a principle of war of modern military code: 'Morale is the most important single battle winning factor in a war'. Help by the angels was promised by Allah during the battle of Uhad also but again "only as a message of good cheer" – Surah 'Ale `Imran Verses

123-126 (these are being quoted here in order to maintain continuity of the subject.)

h.   Clemency and leniency is advised in dealing with captives of war who have to be released as grace or on ransom, which may include exchange of prisoners of war. Killing them is not any part of the Ordinance of Allah. More on this under Surah Muhammad and Al Maida.

Text of the relevant verses:

V – 5

"Even as thy Lord caused thee (Muhammad) to go forth from thy home with the Truth, and lo! a party of the believers were averse (to it)."

V – 6

"Disputing with thee of the Truth after it had been made manifest, as if they were being driven to death visible."

V – 7

"And when Allah promised you one of the two bands (of the enemy) that it should be yours, and ye longed that other than the armed one might be yours. And Allah willed that He should cause the Truth to triumph by His words, and cut the root of the disbelievers;"

V – 8

"That He might cause the Truth to triumph and bring vanity to naught, however much the guilty might oppose;"

V – 9

"When ye sought help of your Lord and He answered you (saying): I will help you with a thousand of the angels, rank on rank."

V - 10

"Allah appointed it only as good tidings, and that your hearts thereby might be at rest. Victory cometh only by the help of Allah. Lo! Allah is Mighty, Wise."

V – 17

"Ye (Muslims) slew them not, but Allah slew them. And thou (Muhammad) threwest not when thou didst throw, but Allah threw, that He might test the believers by a fair test from Him. Lo! Allah is Hearer, Knower."

V – 18

"That (is the case); and (know) that Allah (it is) Who maketh weak the plan of disbelievers."

V – 19

"(O Qureysh!) If ye sought a judgment, now hath the judgment come unto you. And if ye cease (from persecuting the believers) it will be better for you, but if ye return (to the attack) We also shall return. And your host will avail you naught, however numerous it be, and (know) that Allah is with the believers (in His Guidance)."

Surah 'Ale `Imran Verses 123-126

V – 123
"Allah had already given you the victory at Badr, when ye were contemptible. So observe your duty to Allah in order that ye may be thankful."

V – 124
"When thou didst say unto the believers: Is it not sufficient for you that your Lord should support you with three thousand angels sent down (to your help)?"

V – 125
"Nay, but if ye persevere, and keep from evil, and (the enemy) attack you suddenly, your Lord will help you with five thousand angels sweeping on."

V – 126
"Allah ordained this only as a message of good cheer for you, and that thereby your hearts might be at rest - Victory cometh only from Allah, the Mighty, the Wise –"

Surah Al-'Anfal continues

V – 38

"Tell those who disbelieve that if they cease (from persecution of believers) that which is past will be forgiven them; but if they return (thereto) then the example of the men of old hath already gone (before them, for a warning)."

V – 39

"And fight them until persecution is no more, and religion is all for Allah. But if they cease, then lo! Allah is Seer of what they do."

V – 40

"And if they turn away, then know that Allah is your Befriender - a Transcendent Patron, a Transcendent Helper!"

V – 43

"When Allah showed them unto thee (O Muhammad) in thy dream as few in number, and if He had shown them to thee as many, ye (Muslims) would have faltered and would have quarrelled over the affair. But Allah saved (you). Lo! He knoweth what is in the breasts (of men)."

V – 44

"And when He made you (Muslims), when ye

met (them), see them with your eyes as few, and lessened you in their eyes, (it was) that Allah might conclude a thing that must be done. Unto Allah all things are brought back."

V – 45
"O ye who believe! When ye meet an army, hold firm and think of Allah much, that ye may be successful."

V – 46
"And obey Allah and His messenger, and dispute not one with another lest ye falter and your strength depart from you; but be steadfast! Lo! Allah is with the steadfast."

V – 47
"Be not as those who came forth from their dwellings boastfully and to be seen of men, and debar (men) from the way of Allah, while Allah is surrounding all they do."

V – 56
"Those of them with whom thou madest a treaty, and then at every opportunity they break their treaty, and they keep not duty (to Allah)."

V – 57
"If thou comest on them in the war, deal with them

so as to strike fear in those who are behind them, that haply they may remember."

V – 58
"And if thou fearest treachery from any folk, then throw back to them (their treaty) fairly. Lo! Allah loveth not the treacherous."

V – 60
"Make ready for them all thou canst of (armed) force and of horses tethered, that thereby ye may dismay the enemy of Allah and your enemy, and others beside them whom ye know not. Allah knoweth them. Whatsoever ye spend in the way of Allah it will be repaid to you in full, and ye will not be wronged."

V – 61
"And if they incline to peace, incline thou also to it, and trust in Allah. Lo! He, even He, is the Hearer, the Knower."

V – 62
"And if they would deceive thee, then lo! Allah is Sufficient for thee. He it is Who supporteth thee with His help and with the believers,"

V – 67

"It is not for any prophet to have captives until he hath made slaughter in the land. Ye desire the lure of this world and Allah desireth (for you) the Hereafter, and Allah is Mighty, Wise."

V – 68

"Had it not been for an ordinance of Allah which had gone before, an awful doom had come upon you on account of what ye took."

V – 69

"Now enjoy what ye have won, as lawful and good, and keep your duty to Allah. Lo! Allah is Forgiving, Merciful."

V – 70

"O Prophet! Say unto those captives who are in your hands: If Allah knoweth any good in your hearts He will give you better than that which hath been taken from you, and will forgive you. Lo! Allah is Forgiving, Merciful."

V – 71

"And if they would betray thee, they betrayed Allah before, and He gave (thee) power over them. Allah is Knower, Wise."

Surah Muhammad (47)

V – 4

"Now when ye meet in battle those who disbelieve, then it is smiting of the necks until, when ye have routed them, then making fast of bonds; and afterward either grace or ransom till the war lay down its burdens. That (is the ordinance). And if Allah willed He could have punished them (without you) but (thus it is ordained) that He may try some of you by means of others. And those who are slain in the way of Allah, He rendereth not their actions vain."

12. The above verse was revealed before the battle of Badr while verse 67 of Al Anfal was revealed as a sequel to Badr. Neither of these advise killing of the captives of war. There is no other injunction in the Qur'an advising any different treatment of the captives. Tales and stories may abound but it is inconceivable that the Prophet would allow a clear Ordinance of Allah to be relegated to a supposed edict of 'Torah' regarding captives of war. The case in point is the Jewish tribe of Bani Qureiza who, having been besieged for nearly a month, offered a conditional surrender, as a result of which all their men were allegedly slaughtered with the consent of the Prophet on the basis of a decision by their former tribal chief who had converted to Islam and was acceptable to them as an arbiter. This

cannot be accepted at its face value being against the earlier and later practices of the Prophet. It is surprising that matter of the indiscriminate killing under question has been accepted (or agreed upon) almost like a gospel truth, in all the 'tafaseer' that I have been reading to help me understand teachings of the Qur'an (Javed Ahmed Ghamidi has also gone along – Renaissance June 2002, p-33). But the truth is,

"... Ye slew some, and some ye captured" (V – 26 Al-Ahzab)

And the two actions happen in a battle and not in an abject surrender. Also that 'ye' stands for the fighters of the Muslim force and not for the Prophet. Earlier on, when the Jewish tribes were punished on similar grounds they were simply banished from the area. However, the crime of Bani Qureiza was much graver. They were war traitors and rebels, and their crime was high treason against Madina while it was blockaded, calling for death punishment by any standards, then and today. Yet indiscriminate blood bath and enslaving of all their women and children would not earn laurels for the Prophet and, indeed, would be a highly retrograde step. For some support to this point of view let me quote paragraph 30 of the book 'Critical Exposition of the Popular Jehad' by Maulvi (or Maulana) Chiragh Ali.

"The Bani Koreiza had surrendered themselves to the judgment of Saad, an Awsite of their allies, Bani Aws. To this Muhammad agreed. Saad decreed that the male captives should be slaughtered. Muhammad disapproving the judgment, remarked to Saad: "Thou hast decided like the decision of a king," meaning thereby a despotic monarch - the best authentic tradition in Bokhari (Kitab-ul-Jihad)"; adding further that 'Muslim' has also used this word 'Malik' in his collection.

Maulana Mufti Muhammad Shafi has indicated in 'Maarif ul Qur'an' Volume 7 Page 118 last line (translation) – 'Out of those proposed (/marked) to be slaughtered, a few who converted to Islam were granted amnesty and freed'. I therefore surmise that only the ring leaders might have been killed.

Surah 'Ale 'Imran (3) And Surah An-Nisa' (4).

13. Most verses pertaining to the topic of Jihad or Qital in these Surah are in the backdrop of the battle of Uhad. In the third year of Hijra the Meccans came out against Al-Madinah with an army of three thousand men to avenge their defeat at Badr in the previous year and to wipe out the Muslims. The Prophet moved forth with an army of one thousand, but a big group of lukewarm Muslims – later pronounced 'munafeqeen' (the hypocrites) – pulled out of the force on the pretext that their advice to

fight remaining close to home had been rejected, thus putting their lives in undue danger; later on, some of them took the plea that they thought there would be no fighting that day. The Muslims suffered a reverse in this battle and barely avoided a defeat. Seventy brave companions of the Prophet embraced martyrdom with many wounded, including the Prophet. The hypocrites rejoiced for not having joined the battle and continued their propaganda campaign in conjunction with the now openly defiant Jewish tribes, who sent their emissaries to Meccan oligarchy to evolve a joint strategy against the Islamic order, even declaring they considered idolatry better religion than Al-Islam. Such were the circumstances of strict Qur'anic edicts against the hypocrites and renegades to warn them of severe punishment as deserved by deserters. And yet exceptions were made to an extent that very few of the culprits were taken to task.

14. Surah 'Ale 'Imran (3). Dealing with the renegades it is emphasized that they shall stand cursed and doomed except for those who repent. But if they grow violent in disbelief and die in disbelief, no amount of gold (i.e. nothing in material terms) would ransom them. And Allah will replace them with God fearing believers. No punishment is specified for them in this corporal world, for only God knows any disbeliever who may repent and become a believer (till his last breath) and be

forgiven by the Merciful God Who has further ordained that no human being shall be killed for other than manslaughter or for spreading corruption in the earth (Al-Maida V-32; V-54 also being relevant here is quoted below).

V – 84

"Say (O Muhammad): We believe in Allah and that which is revealed unto us and that which was revealed unto Abraham and Ishmael and Isaac and Jacob and the tribes, and that which was vouchsafed unto Moses and Jesus and the prophets from their Lord. We make no distinction between any of them, and unto Him we have surrendered."

V - 85

"And whoso seeketh as religion other than the Surrender (to Allah) it will not be accepted from him, and he will be a loser in the Hereafter."

V - 86

"How shall Allah guide a people who disbelieved after their belief and (after) they bore witness that the messenger is true and after clear proofs (of Allah's Sovereignty) had come unto them. And Allah guideth not wrongdoing folk."

V – 87

"As for such, their guerdon is that on them rests the curse of Allah and of angels and of men combined."

V - 88

"They will abide therein. Their doom will not be lightened, neither will they be reprieved;"

V - 89

"Save those who afterward repent and do right. Lo! Allah is Forgiving, Merciful."

V - 90

"Lo! Those who disbelieve after their (profession of) belief, and afterward grow violent in disbelief: their repentance will not be accepted. And such are those who are astray."

V - 91

"Lo! those who disbelieve, and die in disbelief, the (whole) earth full of gold would not be accepted from such an one if it were offered as a ransom (for his soul). Theirs will be a painful doom and they will have no helpers."

Surah Al-Maida (5)

V – 32

"For that cause We decreed for the Children of Israel that whosoever killeth a human being for other than manslaughter or corruption in the earth, it shall be as if he had killed all mankind, and whoso saveth the life of one, it shall be as if he had saved the life of all mankind. Our messengers came unto them of old with clear proofs (of Allah's Sovereignty), but afterwards lo! many of them became prodigals in the earth."

V – 54

"O ye who believe! Whoso of you becometh a renegade from his religion, (know that in his stead) Allah will bring a people whom He loveth and who love Him, humble toward believers, stern toward disbelievers, striving in the way of Allah, and fearing not the blame of any blamer. Such is the grace of Allah which He giveth unto whom He will. Allah is All-Embracing, All-Knowing."

15. Surah An-Nisa' (4).

a. Dealing with the Pagans of Mecca it is emphasized that they must be stopped from persecuting the feeble group of believers still in the town,seeking your help and protection.

b. The believers are told to beware of the hypocrites who would try to entice them back. Those turning to active hostility have to be dealt with harshly, but not indiscriminately, taking full care that you don't kill a believer even by mistake; or else you would even have to pay blood money.

c. No hostile action is to be taken against those

aligned with groups in covenant with you as well as those who wish to stay neutral and offer you peace.

d. Verses 137-138 touch upon the renegades and hypocrites.

V - 74

"Let those fight in the way of Allah who sell the life of this world for the other. Whoso fighteth in the way of Allah, be he slain or be he victorious, on him We shall bestow a vast reward."

V - 75

"How should ye not fight for the cause of Allah and of the feeble among men and of the women and the children who are crying: Our Lord! Bring us forth from out this town of which the people are oppressors! Oh, give us from thy presence some protecting friend! Oh, give us from Thy presence some defender!"

V - 84

"So fight (O Muhammad) in the way of Allah - Thou art not taxed (with the responsibility for anyone) except thyself - and urge on the believers. Peradventure Allah will restrain the might of those who disbelieve. Allah is stronger in might and stronger in inflicting punishment."

V - 88

"What aileth you that ye are become two parties regarding the hypocrites, when Allah cast them back (to disbelief) because of what they earned? Seek ye to guide him whom Allah hath sent astray? He whom Allah sendeth astray, for him thou (O MUhammad) canst not find a road."

V - 89

"They long that ye should disbelieve even as they disbelieve, that ye may be upon a level (with them). So choose not friends from them till they forsake their homes in the way of Allah; if they turn back (to enmity) then take them and kill them wherever ye find them, and choose no friend nor helper from among them,"

V - 90

"Except those who seek refuge with a people between whom and you there is a covenant, or (those who) come unto you because their hearts forbid them to make war on you or make war on their own folk. Had Allah willed He could have given them power over you so that assuredly they would have fought you. So, if they hold aloof from you and wage not war against you and offer you peace, Allah alloweth you no way against them."

V – 91

"Ye will find others who desire that they should

have security from you, and security from their own folk. So often as they are returned to hostility they are plunged therein. If they keep not aloof from you nor offer you peace nor hold their hands, then take them and kill them wherever ye find them. Against such We have given you clear warrant."

V - 92

"It is not for a believer to kill a believer unless (it be) by mistake. He who hath killed a believer by mistake must set free a believing slave, and pay the blood-money to the family of the slain, unless they remit it as a charity. If he (the victim) be of a people hostile unto you, and he is a believer, then (the penance is) to set free a believing slave. And if he cometh of a folk between whom and you there is a covenant, then the blood-money must be paid unto his folk and (also) a believing slave must be set free. And whoso hath not the wherewithal must fast two consecutive months. A penance from Allah. Allah is Knower, Wise."

V – 93

"Whoso slayeth a believer of set purpose, his reward is hell for ever. Allah is wroth against him and He hath cursed him and prepared for him an awful doom."

V - 94

"O ye who believe! When ye go forth (to fight) in

the way of Allah, be careful to discriminate, and say not unto one who offereth you peace: "Thou art not a believer," seeking the chance profits of this life (so that ye may despoil him). With Allah are plenteous spoils. Even thus (as he now is) were ye before; but Allah hath since then been gracious unto you. Therefore take care to discriminate. Allah is ever Informed of what ye do."

V - 137

"Lo! those who believe, then disbelieve and then (again) believe, then disbelieve, and then increase in disbelief, Allah will never pardon them, nor will He guide them unto a way."

V - 138

"Bear unto the hypocrites the tidings that for them there is a painful doom;"

V - 139

"Those who choose disbelievers for their friends instead of believers! Do they look for power at their hands? Lo! all power appertaineth to Allah."

Surah Al Tauba (9).

16. Having migrated to Madina under compulsion, the Prophet signed treaties of mutual alliance and neutrality with the Jews of Madina and some Pagan tribes. However, while Muslims remained

faithful to the agreed terms, the opposite side continued to violate the treaties whenever it suited them. The Peace Accord of Hudaebia could be considered 'Mother of all Treaties' signed between the Prophet and the Quraish of Mecca, each signing independent treaties of alliance with other groups as well. Surah Al-Tauba was revealed in the backdrop of the breach of this treaty by the tribe of Bani Bakr allied with and openly supported by the Quraish against the Muslims' allied tribe of Bani Khuza'a. Unable to fight back the ruthless offensive, the latter took refuge in the Sacred Mosque, but were attacked there also and many of them killed mercilessly. Their emissaries took a plaint to the Prophet and sought action as per the agreed terms. The Prophet, deciding to take a strong punitive action, mobilized a force of ten thousand fighters and swiftly moved to conquer Mecca, which eventually offered a docile surrender. However, as a last ditch effort, a strong group of Pagan tribes led by Bani Hawazin and Bani Saqeef again joined hands to attack and take back Mecca but the Prophet pre-empted this by himself moving with a large force against them. A decisive battle took place at Hunaen in which the Muslim fighters initially suffered a reverse but, on a specific call by the Prophet, a dedicated group of his valiant fighters saved the day.

17. While the whole account of Hudaebia from the

selection of the timing of the pilgrimage during the month prohibited for war putting the Quraish in a dilemma to deny this universally recognized sacred mission, till the signing of the Accord and its aftermath in terms of the fast spread of Islam on account of the ensuing peaceful conditions can, on its own, be termed 'Strategy' par excellence. But, observing at a broader canvas, the chain of events from the episode of Hudaebia to the successful pre-emptive strike against the combine of the Jews and Bani Ghatafan with final reduction of Khaeber, violation of the treaty of Hudaebia by the Meccans and the Prophet's reaction in terms of a strong show of force resulting in docile surrender of Mecca, the magnanimity displayed in declaring general amnesty for all and sundry neutralizing their antagonism for that time which, in turn, allowed the Prophet to swiftly move for the decisive battle of Hunaen; taken altogether can be rightly termed 'Grand Strategy' which, in the modern military parlance, means to so integrate the military strategy with statesmanship that resort to war is rendered unnecessary or is undertaken with maximum chance of victory. Here allow me to add that the Prophet, right from the start, has had the advantage in terms of pre-action Guidance and post-action Approval of many of his actions by the All Knowing Who owned up as His Own some of the actions of the Prophet like a handful of dust heralded towards the enemy, supposedly and admittedly, reaching the eyes of enemy fighters, and declaring an apparent loss of face at Hudaebia as an Open or Signal Victory - so proved beyond question by the subsequent events.

18. Surah Al-Tauba is seen to have broadly two parts. Verses 1 – 28 relate to the background events covered above while the remaining Surah primarily covers another landmark campaign to Tabuk a far off area in the North of Arabia, touching fringes of the Christian Byzantine Empire. On learning that the Qaisar of Rome was gathering forces for a big putsch against the Islamic confederation, the Prophet rallied an unprecedented army of thirty thousand fighters and moved off to Tabuk in circumstances clearly unfavorable in many respects but which forced a change of mind on the part of the enemy who quietly dispersed. The Prophet extended his stay there to twenty days during which a large group of tribes (Christians, Jews and Idolatrous Arabs), hitherto under the influence of the Romans, pledged fidelity to the Islamic state of Madina and agreed to pay 'Jizya' (Verse 29). Considering the military and religio-politico-diplomatic results of the campaign, it can be termed a masterstroke in strategy where a strong timely maneuver determined the desired result of thwarting warlike moves of the enemy.

19. Coming now to the sacred text of the verses of Surah

Al-Tauba, some injunctions here appear rather threatening and, are possibly therefore, made a subject of much criticism by the non-adherent scholars of Al-Islam. To be able to understand the true import of the stern commandments, so to say, contained in Surah Al-Tauba, I would sound a note of caution not to decontextualize the text, i.e. we have to carefully read every word and every line of the sacred text, keeping in mind the chain of the background events, in particular the repeated violation of the treaties on the part of the idolaters in total disregard of their covenants. So it opens with a proclamation from Allah and His messenger that they are free from obligation towards those of the idolaters who have violated the Treaty (in this case the Accord of Hudaebia). It is further proclaimed to all that indeed Allah and His messenger are free from obligation to all the idolaters with whom the Muslims had made treaties of mutual alliance or neutrality, because whenever the former had an upper hand, they broke their compacts. A specific exception is made for those who were confederates of the Muslims signing treaty at the Inviolable Place of Worship, advising both parties to honour their commitments till the completion of their terms. The violators of the treaties are given four months to repent and make amends. After comprehensively detailing indictments against them, the kind of treatment they deserve is spelt out --- "slay them ...". And yet, if they repent, "then leave their way". And yet again, if any show inclination to faith, provide them protection and guidance in matters of religion. Then let them decide for themselves. Verses 1 to 18 (and infact even beyond) form an interesting treatise barely needing elaboration.

Verse 29 covers another sensitive subject 'Jizya' which will be dealt with in some detail at the end.

V – 1
"Freedom from obligation (is proclaimed) from Allah and His messenger toward those of the idolaters with whom ye made a treaty."

V – 2
"Travel freely in the land four months, and know that ye cannot escape Allah and that Allah will confound the disbelievers (in His Guidance)."

V – 3
"And a proclamation from Allah and His messenger to all men on the day of the Greater Pilgrimage that Allah is free from obligation to the idolaters, and (so is) His messenger. So, if ye repent, it will be better for you; but if ye are averse, then know that ye cannot escape Allah. Give tidings (O Muhammad) of a painful doom to those who disbelieve,"

V – 4

"Excepting those of the idolaters with whom ye (Muslims) have a treaty, and who have since abated nothing of your right nor have supported anyone against you. (As for these), fulfil their treaty to them till their term. Lo! Allah loveth those who keep their duty (unto Him)."

V – 5

"Then, when the sacred months have passed, slay the idolaters wherever ye find them, and take them (captive), and besiege them, and prepare for them each ambush. But if they repent and establish worship and pay the poor-due, then leave their way free. Lo! Allah is Forgiving, Merciful."

V – 6

"And if anyone of the idolaters seeketh thy protection (O Muhammad), then protect him so that he may hear the Word of Allah, and afterward convey him to his place of safety. That is because they are a folk who know not."

V – 7

"How can there be a treaty with Allah and with His messenger for the idolaters save those with whom ye made a treaty at the Inviolable Place of Worship? So long as they are true to you, be true to them. Lo! Allah loveth those who keep their duty."

V – 8

"How (can there be any treaty for the others) when, if they have the upper hand of you, they regard not pact nor honour in respect of you? They satisfy you with their mouths the while their hearts refuse. And most of them are wrongdoers."

V – 9

"They have purchased with the revelations of Allah a little gain, so they debar (men) from His way. Lo! evil is that which they are wont to do."

V – 10

"And they observe toward a believer neither pact nor honour. These are they who are transgressors."

V – 11

"But if they repent and establish worship and pay the poor-due, then are they your brethren in religion. We detail Our revelations for a people who have knowledge."

V – 12

"And if they break their pledges after their treaty (hath been made with you) and assail your religion, then fight the heads of disbelief - Lo! they have no binding oaths - in order that they may desist."

V – 13

"Will ye not fight a folk who broke their solemn pledges, and purposed to drive out the messenger and did attack you first? What! Fear ye them? Now Allah hath more right that ye should fear Him, if ye are believers"

V – 14

"Fight them! Allah will chastise them at your hands, and He will lay them low and give you victory over them, and He will heal the breasts of folk who are believers."

V – 15

"And He will remove the anger of their hearts. Allah relenteth toward whom He will. Allah is Knower, Wise."

V – 16

"Or deemed ye that ye would be left (in peace) when Allah yet knoweth not those of you who strive, choosing for familiar none save Allah and His messenger and the believers? Allah is Informed of what ye do."

V – 17

"It is not for the idolaters to tend Allah's sanctuaries, bearing witness against themselves of disbelief. As for such, their works are vain and in the Fire they will abide."

V – 18

"He only shall tend Allah's sanctuaries who believeth in Allah and the Last Day and observeth proper worship and payeth the poor-due and feareth none save Allah. For such (only) is it possible that they can be of the rightly guided."

V – 19

"Count ye the slaking of a pilgrim's thirst and tendance of the Inviolable Place of Worship as (equal to the worth of) him who believeth in Allah and the Last Day, and striveth in the way of Allah? They are not equal in the sight of Allah. Allah guideth not wrongdoing folk."

V – 20

"Those who believe, and have left their homes and striven with their wealth and their lives in Allah's way are of much greater worth in Allah's sight. These are they who are triumphant."

V – 28

"O ye who believe! The idolaters only are unclean. So let them not come near the Inviolable Place of Worship after this their year. If ye fear poverty (from the loss of their merchandise) Allah shall preserve you of His bounty if He will. Lo! Allah is Knower, Wise."

V – 29

"Fight against such of those who have been given the Scripture as believe not in Allah nor the Last Day, and forbid not that which Allah hath forbidden by His messenger, and follow not the Religion of Truth, until they pay the tribute readily, being brought low."

V – 30

"And the Jews say: Ezra is the son of Allah, and the Christians say: The Messiah is the son of Allah. That is their saying with their mouths. They imitate the saying of those who disbelieved of old. Allah (Himself) fighteth against them. How perverse are they!"

V – 31

"They have taken as lords beside Allah their rabbis and their monks and the Messiah son of Mary, when they were bidden to worship only One Allah. There is no Allah save Him. Be He Glorified from all that they ascribe as partner (unto Him)!"

V – 33

"He it is Who hath sent His messenger with the guidance and the Religion of Truth, that He may cause it to prevail over all religion, however much the idolaters may be averse."

V – 34

"O ye who believe! Lo! many of the (Jewish) rabbis and the (Christian) monks devour the wealth of mankind wantonly and debar (men) from the way of Allah. They who hoard up gold and silver and spend it not in the way of Allah, unto them give tidings (O Muhammad) of a painful doom,"

V – 35

"On the day when it will (all) be heated in the fire of hell, and their foreheads and their flanks and their backs will be branded therewith (and it will be said unto them): Here is that which ye hoarded for yourselves. Now taste of what ye used to hoard."

V – 73

"Know they not that Allah knoweth both their secret and the thought that they confide, and that Allah is the Knower of Things Hidden?"

V – 88

"But the messenger and those who believe with him strive with their wealth and their lives. Such are they for whom are the good things. Such are they who are the successful."

V – 111

"Lo! Allah hath bought from the believers their

lives and their wealth because the Garden will be theirs: they shall fight in the way of Allah and shall slay and be slain. It is a promise which is binding on Him in the Torah and the Gospel and the Qur'an. Who fulfilleth His covenant better than Allah? Rejoice then in your bargain that ye have made, for that is the supreme triumph."

V – 123
"O ye who believe! Fight those of the disbelievers who are near to you, and let them find harshness in you, and know that Allah is with those who keep their duty (unto Him)."

20. Having carefully read and re-read Surah Al-Tauba one can easily notice that, even on its face value, only a part of verse (No. 5) may appear to have a threatening tone. Even so, it applies only to violators of a treaty (Accord of Hudaebia) as made clear in verses 2 & 3 which also serve a notice of four months to the culprits to repent; making further clear (verse 4) that the stern edicts do not apply to those idolaters who have not violated the terms of their treaty. From here on it is all exhortation in different forms inspiring and advising the Muslims to be ready to take on the incorrigible offenders. It is worth considering if verse 5 can connect with verses 17 & 18 where the idolaters are being barred from the Sacred Precincts (possibly, in the process,

denying them some pecuniary benefits) with a clear warning that no leniency shall be shown in this regard, and that they should, therefore, better stay far away, or face the consequences. Reading through whole of the Surah, I could not find any other strict edicts like that in verse 5. However, I did stop at verses 111 & 123, and noticed these to be a bit more incisive but definitely not suggesting to initiate unprovoked hostilities and aggression. Allow me to say that we have to ponder and deliberate on the Qur'anic injunctions with open minds casting aside preconceived ideas and all kinds of prejudices. This is the only way to draw right conclusions for our guidance.

21. Coming to verse 29, it is criticized, perhaps purely, on the face value of the word or term Jizya —tribute required to be paid by non muslims living in an Islamic state. They are allowed freedom of religion and conscience as well as civil rights enjoyed by the Muslims, but they shall be governed by laws of the Islamic state. The said verse refers specifically to the 'People of the Book' who paid lip service to their religion without following its basic tenets, even like the belief in God and the Hereafter, and were, therefore, treated as non believers and placed at par with idolaters. Indictment of these 'People of the Scripture' is aptly spelt out in verses 30, 31, 34 and 35.

V – 29

"Fight against such of those who have been given the Scripture as believe not in Allah nor the Last Day, and forbid not that which Allah hath forbidden by His messenger, and follow not the Religion of Truth, until they pay the tribute readily, being brought low."

V – 30

"And the Jews say: Ezra is the son of Allah, and the Christians say: The Messiah is the son of Allah. That is their saying with their mouths. They imitate the saying of those who disbelieved of old. Allah (Himself) fighteth against them. How perverse are they!"

V – 31

"They have taken as lords beside Allah their rabbis and their monks and the Messiah son of Mary, when they were bidden to worship only One Allah. There is no Allah save Him. Be He Glorified from all that they ascribe as partner (unto Him)!"

V – 34

"O ye who believe! Lo! many of the (Jewish) rabbis and the (Christian) monks devour the wealth of mankind wantonly and debar (men) from the way of Allah. They who hoard up gold and silver and spend it not in the way of Allah, unto them give tidings (O Muhammad) of a painful doom,"

V – 35

"On the day when it will (all) be heated in the fire of hell, and their foreheads and their flanks and their backs will be branded therewith (and it will be said unto them): Here is that which ye hoarded for yourselves. Now taste of what ye used to hoard."

22. A comprehensive treatise on the subject of Jizya is given as a sequel to Surah Al-Tauba in Vol 2 (Pages 121-122) of 'Tarajaman ul Qur'an' by Maulana Abul-Ul Kamal Azad. He has on page 122 quoted a succinct opinion of a French scholar Mounsieur Lebon who, while commenting on the practice of Jizya says (translation) – "In the Islamic state, the non muslim minorities got all that any nation can have, however they did not have one right – to be Caliph in that state". The Islamic scholar Abdullah Yusuf Ali has summarized important elements of the concept of Jizya in his work 'The Holy Qur'an – Text, Translation And Commentary' Vol 1 (Notes No. 1281 & 1282), parts of which are quoted below:

Note 1281 – "Jizya: the root meaning is compensation. The derived meaning, which became the technical meaning, was a poll-tax levied from those who did not accept Islam, but were willing to live under the protection of Islam, and were thus tacitly willing to submit to its ideals being enforced in the Muslim State, saving only their personal liberty of conscience as regarded themselves. There was no amount fixed for it and in any case it was merely symbolical, -- an acknowledgment that those whose religion was tolerated would in their turn not interfere with the preaching and progress of Islam. The tax varied in amount, and there were exemptions for the poor, for females and children (according to Abu Hanifa), for slaves, and for monks and hermits. Being a tax on able-bodied males of military age, it was in a sense a commutation for military services."

Note 1282 – "An Yadin" (literally, from the hand) has been variously interpreted. The hand being the symbol of power and authority, I accept the interpretation "in token of willing submission". The Jizya was thus partly a commutation for military service, but as the amount was insignificant and the exemptions numerous, its symbolic character predominated."

In the present day democratic political dispensation, religious minorities are expected to enjoy equal civil rights and religious freedom (but for the undeclared prejudices, vested interests and hidden agendas, as well as the subjugation of people through military occupation). Indeed we can agree the Jizya clause may no more be applicable as would be the case with 'Slavery' and 'Spoils of War' where, in the present day scenario, it will be hilarious to imagine fighters of the victor force claiming seizure of tanks, artillery pieces, fighter jets (and how can you rule out small tactical nuclear devices) and all with respective crews!

23. We have gone over nearly all the verses directly related to the subject of Jihad in the Qur'an (the count happens to come to one hundred). After a deep and objective analysis (as much as I found it possible on my part) of all the edicts and exhortational injunctions contained in these verses, I am constrained to emphasize that Islam does not approve of initiation of hostilities and aggression (2:190) as also proselytizing through persecution in any form whatsoever. Indeed the Qur'an terms persecution, particularly in relation to religion, worse than slaughter (2:191, 2:217) ordaining further that such persecution must be resolutely fought against and eliminated (2:193, 8:39). Also that, while fighting oppression and injustice, transgression and excess in revenge is not allowed (2:194, 22:60). And if the enemy desists or shows inclination towards peace, such overtures should be reciprocated (2:193, 8:61). Having recapitulated briefly the injunctions of the Qur'an on the subject, we need to dwell in some more detail on a few of these verses with important implications:

Surah Al Hajj V-39 is the first verse revealed giving sanction to the Muslims to fight because they had been wronged, qualifying it with the exhortation that "Allah indeed is able to give them victory". This is closely linked to the next verse (No. 40) which describes the wrong done to them – "having been driven from their homes unjustly only because they said: Our Lord is Allah". These two verses read in conjunction with verse 22:60 ("retaliate with the like of that you were made to suffer - ") and 2:191 (" slay them wherever you find them, and drive them out -- ") appear to complete the cycle. So, logically, the displaced Muslims had sanction to even rehabilitate themselves back onto their own homes and hearths. They didn't however, do that; but from around the time of fall of Mecca persecution of "the feeble ..." (V – 75, Al-Nisa) had stopped. This leads me to believe that it is a religious duty of the believers to wage perpetual struggle – " And strive for Allah with the endeavor which is His right ..." (22:78), and eliminate all forms of oppression and iniquity with the aim of establishing Allah's religion with all its manifestations. That there must not be persecution suggests that belief and faith have to come as a matter of free will and call of conscience, and not under any kind of coercion and physical threat such as - at the point of a sword, so to say. Here we are at a delicate point of discussion because faith itself is God's most precious blessing and the quality of our effort shall depend upon the quality of our faith and guidance provided by God totally in accordance with His Will and Purpose.

Briefly stated our duty is to make our best effort to understand what is required of us as laid down in the revealed book, the Qur'an and act upon it with maximum sincerity.

24. The ground reality, however, is rather discouraging. Take for example the tenet of Jihad. Totally misunderstood, it is being relentlessly practiced by individuals as well as splinter groups almost in all parts of the planet causing indiscriminate killings and massive destruction being termed Islamic Terrorism by the antagonists. Hundreds of thousands of innocent people including women and children have lost their lives at the hands of such terrorist activities because the perpetrators as well as their sponsors and instigators appear to have nothing to do with the edict "whosoever killeth a human being for other than manslaughter and corruption in the earth, it shall be as if he had killed all mankind and whoso saveth ..." (5:32). And the corruptors here should include rapists and molesters (in particular those targeting minors and killing them in most cases), dacoits, mafias, traitors, groups putting up armed resistance to governments elected through recognized fair electoral process, dictators of all hues, persecutors and oppressors on the basis of religion, incestuous (and gays if you like); punishment for each category being decided through legislation – death or cutting off of hands and feet of opposite sides being the

maximum punishment in the Islamic Law likely to be fully endorsed at least by those who have suffered at the hands of such perpetrators.

25. Another area of concern here is the fact that the Jihadi cadres are no more the relatively uneducated lot that has come out of the 'Madrasas'. These now include formally educated young as well as elderly people who claim to know what religion demands and that they are only following its precepts in practical terms ready to risk their lives for "Islam is to prevail over all religions" (9:33). Tehrik-e-Taliban Pakistan (TTP) the lead organization here have plonked themselves in the Northern mountainous areas of the country and appear to have tentacles spread all over claiming responsibility for most of the carnage events including terror attacks during the election campaign, and further open threats as well as earlier mass killings of perhaps the most peaceful members of the Shia community, not forgetting the later abominal chain of the merciless and senseless target killings that followed. They consider our present political dispensation Un-Islamic. They want 'Khilafat' under the aegis of an 'Ameer Ul Momineen' who will enforce 'Sharia', and chase all non adherents to the end of the earth to proselytize them or they pay Jizya if they happen to be People of the Book. This view is clearly challengeable and would have entailed endless discussions ever since

the Prophet breathed his last. The only way for us, therefore, is to see the matter in the light of the Qur'anic injunctions because these cannot be imagined to have been deviated from in the least by the Prophet.

26. I am a military man and having studied the battles the Prophet had to fight, I find these were essentially of defensive nature. He never initiated hostilities, did not exceed in revenge, and never tried to convert non believers under coercion of any kind, the ultimate form of which would have been battle field, where injunction against those who simply wish to stay neutral is:

V 4:90
"... So, if they hold aloof from you and wage not war against you and offer you peace, Allah alloweth you no way against them".

Captives of Badr, the most vulnerable category for that moment, were all released free or on symbolic ransom including what may invite laughter if not disbelief – impart a little of formal education to a certain number of the illiterate among the Muslim community. If enemy showed inclination to peace the Prophet came more than half way but he did not forgive treachery and did not hesitate on a preemptive action to forestall offensive moves by the enemy which could impact on his mission of peaceful preaching. To judge the veracity of these assertions, a brief look on the battles:-

a. Badr (1 H). This is the only battle where most of the non-muslim scholars have blamed the Prophet for deliberately provoking his foe into action because he planned to despoil the big trade caravan of the Quraish as one may, on the face of it, surmise. This is disproved in view of the following facts:

i. To the utter chagrin of the Meccan Patriarchy, the Prophet escaped their combined murderous attack and made it to the security of Madina. The Prophet was ever vigilant to any inroads by the enemy and would send out scouting missions to obtain information about enemy intentions as well as to maintain moral ascendency and display a modicum of belligerency. This, in the present day military terminology, is called 'Patrolling'.

ii. These missions or patrols normally comprised the emigrant 'companions' because the 'helpers' ex Madina had pledged to protect the Prophet against enemy onslaughts and not to participate in any offensive action against the Quraish and others. Such missions were not allowed to engage in any fighting except in self defense. As such there was no question of waylaying the trade caravans. And in the case of skirmish at Nakhla during the period prohibited for warfare, the Prophet reproved the mission incharge and paid blood money for one of the fighters killed in the skirmish.

iii. Coming to the big trade caravan led by Abu Sufyan, the allegation that the Prophet planned to despoil it is ludicrous for the simple reason that it would have been considered an offensive action which the Madinites were not pledged to support. Above all, the contemporary evidence (Al-Anfal verses 5-10, 17, 43 & 44) proves that the clash at Badr was a divine plan with sublime aims, and could not have been except as it was.

b. Uhad (3 H). Clearly a defensive battle (para 13).

c. Al-Ahzab or 'The Clans' (5H). Again no question on it being a defensive battle fought against overwhelming odds by digging a ditch (or Trench – Pickthall). A ten thousand strong army comprising fighters of many Bedouin tribes led by Bani Ghatafan with all its branches coming from the North of Madina and the Quraish from the South, all instigated and joined by the Jews from Khaeber, attacked Madina in order to extirpate Muslims. However, not having reckoned with the ditch, they eventually had to lift the siege due to stiff resistance and highly disruptive weather conditions towards the end. A graphic account of this war can be read in verses 9 to 27 of Surah Al-Ahzab. The treacherous violation by the Bani

Qureiza of their alliance with the Prophet and the punishment meted out to them has been covered in para 12 ibid.

d. Reduction of Khaebar (6H). Khaebar was a stronghold of the Jewish tribes of North Arabia and had become a hornests nest for enemies of the Muslims. A bit demoralized but not deterred by the setback at the battle of the ditch, they again instigated Ghatafan to join hands with them for a putsch against Madina to which effect credible intelligence had been pouring in. The Prophet, in the mean time, had signed Peace accord with the Meccans. He, through a bold pre-emption, deploying his force in area between Khaebar and the Ghatafan, denied them coordinated action. While the Jews were subdued fort after fort despite putting up stiff resistance stretched over a month, the Ghatafan could not provide any meaningful help. It is worthwhile to note that we are not here discussing detailed events of the battle but only trying to determine if such a surprise and pre-emptive move against avowed enemies would be in the nature of offensive or defensive action. This is also a reason for rather briefly covering accounts of these battles.

e. Fall of Mecca. Para 16 elucidates the docile surrender of Meccans who knew the attack was coming as punishment for violating a solemn treaty as well as in response to the persecution of the Muslims still in Mecca.

f. Hunaeyn. Para 16 covers this battle as well. When Mecca fell all the people did not convert right away; there were many lukewarm Muslims and even outright hypocrites. Information was also pouring in about the threatening do or die assembly of the warlike tribes Al-Hawazin and Al-Saqeef. Any attack on Mecca at this stage would have resulted in a confusing situation of the battle which could affect the very loyalties of the populace. Here again the Prophet chose to launch a hurried preemptive where a large number of the recent convertees had joined up, and the Muslim army though outnumbering the enemy, for once, yet had to face a serious reverse initially. Verses 25 & 26 of Surah Al-Tauba give a vivid picture of the situation.

g. Tabuk. Covered at length earlier. Last sentence of para 18 sums up the matter.

27. Overall Summary of Campaigns and Skirmishes. Having settled at Madina the Prophet had signed the famous treaty of alliance with the Jews and other tribes there granting them full civil rights including religious freedom. Attitude of the Jews and the lukewarm Muslims remained inconsistent but after the setback to the Muslims at Uhad it became more hostile, even colluding with the forces

inimical to the Muslims. The Prophet had always remained alert to such developments and had been sending out scouting missions in all directions to collect information about intentions and plans of the adversaries. Besides the scouting missions the Prophet had been sending preaching parties to different areas. After the Hudaebia accord this activity became more pronounced and many preaching missions were sent to far off places within Arabia on the request of local tribal leaders. The Prophet also sent similar missions and a few embassies to the Syrian border up North in areas controlled by the Christian tribes under the Roman influence. In some cases, both in the initial stages and later on, members of these missions were killed mercilessly. It became imperative, therefore, to chastise the perpetrators and to deter the potential trouble makers. The scouting missions thus got converted into military campaigns with the basic purpose of show of force or, in present day terms 'to dominate no man's land', in support of the fence sitters in faith.

28. It is clear that hallmark of all the Prophet's actions was his resolve for strong counter measures so that his mission of preaching in peaceful conditions among the Muslim Commonwealth established at Madina was not interrupted. After Hudaebia and, later on the fall of Mecca and defeat of the Pagan tribes at Hunaeyn, in the following two years (9

& 10 H) a large number of deputations came from all over Arabia as well as from the border of Syria and outskirts of Persia to swear allegiance to the Prophet. There is a list of eighty such deputations / embassies in para 31 (page 66) of the Book 'Jihad' referred to earlier on. Many of the chiefs and princes – both Christians and Pagans – intimated, by letter or by embassy, their conversion to Islam. It is an admitted fact that there was not a single case of conversion through any kind of oppressive action in the whole life of the Prophet. He was required only to convey the divine message to all he could reach, in a best possible mode in order to appeal to the hearts and minds of the recipients. He did this in a manner of friendly persuasion and logical arguments so they could ponder and accept these as a matter of call of conscience and free will. No force was to be used for the Prophet had not been sent as a 'keeper' or 'warder' but as a 'messenger', while final guidance and change of the hearts would come as Blessing from God alone:

Verse 2:256
"There is no compulsion in religion. The right direction is henceforth distinct from error. And he who rejecteth false deities and believeth in Allah hath grasped a firm handhold which will never break. Allah is Hearer, Knower."

Verse 4:80

"Whoso obeyeth the messenger hath obeyed Allah, and whoso turneth away: We have not sent thee as a warder over them."

Verse 5:99

"The duty of the messenger is only to convey (the message). Allah knoweth what ye proclaim and what ye hide."

Verse 3:20

"And if they argue with thee, (O Muhammad), say: I have surrendered my purpose to Allah and (so have) those who follow me. And say unto those who have received the Scripture and those who read not: Have ye (too) surrendered? If they surrender, then truly they are rightly guided, and if they turn away, then it is thy duty only to convey the message (unto them). Allah is Seer of (His) bondmen."

Verse 6:107

"Had Allah willed, they had not been idolatrous. We have not set thee as a keeper over them, nor art thou responsible for them."

Verse 24:54

"Say: Obey Allah and obey the messenger. But if ye turn away, then (it is) for him (to do) only that wherewith he hath been charged, and for you (to do) only that wherewith ye have been charged. If ye obey him, ye will go aright. But the messenger hath no other charge than to convey (the message) plainly."

Verse 39:41
"Lo! We have revealed unto thee (Muhammad) the Scripture for mankind with truth. Then whosoever goeth right it is for his soul, and whosoever strayeth, strayeth only to its hurt. And thou art not a warder over them."

Verse 22:78
"And strive for Allah with the endeavor which is His right. He hath chosen you and hath not laid upon you in religion any hardship; the faith of your father Abraham (is yours)...."

29. This brings us face to face with another critical point in our discussion – Faith that God has selected Islam as our Religion and that Al Qur'an, divinely revealed to Prophet Muhammad (PBUH), explains to us what Al-Islam is, the Prophet being the perfect and practical example we are religiously bound to follow. Further on that we have to "Strive for Allah with the endeavor which is His right". As stated earlier this endeavor shall depend on the quality of our faith while God has retained the power of guidance entirely in His own hands. In other words

quality of faith (or the lack of it) of every individual will be as desired by God. It should then be right to say the better the quality of faith of a person the more blessed he should consider himself to be and, as such, be more grateful and more humble, for it is all By the Grace of God. Thus those blessed with Faith should not feel too proud, rather they should try to sincerely share their blessings with others. Sharing of a blessing cannot involve coercion or highhandedness. It should not even come with a condescending and overbearing attitude. It has to come in the form of sincere persuasion based on logic. The important thing is to understand the total picture of your being what you are and what others are. If you can appreciate the fact that you have been endowed with the special blessing of Faith, not necessarily earned by you, you are likely to be modest and more forbearing. We now need to look at the God's Ordinances in this regard. I, with the help of indices in 'Tafheem Ul Qur'an', located nearly forty verses (there will be more if you are interested) altogether on Faith (or Belief), Guidance, Islam. Let us have a look on some of these verses. To save space I have quoted only substantive part in a few, but to understand their real import the text has to be read in full:

Verse 2:253
"Of those messengers, some of whom We have caused to excel others, and of whom there are

some unto whom Allah spake, while some of them He exalted (above others) in degree; and We gave Jesus, son of Mary, clear proofs (of Allah's Sovereignty) and We supported him with the holy Spirit. And if Allah had so willed it, those who followed after them would not have fought one with another after the clear proofs had come unto them. But they differed, some of them believing and some disbelieving. And if Allah had so willed it, they would not have fought one with another; but Allah doeth what He will."

Verse 4:88
"What aileth you that ye are become two parties regarding the hypocrites, when Allah cast them back (to disbelief) because of what they earned? Seek ye to guide him whom Allah hath sent astray? He whom Allah sendeth astray, for him thou (O Muhammad) canst not find a road."

Verse 6:35
"If Allah willed, He could have brought them all together to the guidance - ...."

Verse 6:39
"Those who deny Our revelations are deaf and dumb in darkness. Whom Allah will sendeth astray, and whom He will He placeth on a straight path."

Verse 6:111

"And though We should send down the angels unto them, and the dead should speak unto them, and We should gather against them all things in array, they would not believe unless Allah so willed. Howbeit, most of them are ignorant."

Verse 6:149

"Say - For Allah's is the final argument - Had He willed He could indeed have guided all of you."

Verse 7:155

"……… Thou sendest whom Thou wilt astray and guidest whom Thou wilt: Thou art our Protecting Friend, therefore forgive us and have mercy on us, Thou, the Best of all who show forgiveness."

Verse 7:178

"He whom Allah leadeth, he indeed is led aright, while he whom Allah sendeth astray - they indeed are losers."

Verse 7:186

"Those whom Allah sendeth astray, there is no guide for them. He leaveth them to wander blindly on in their contumacy."

Verse 22:16

"Thus We reveal it as plain revelations, and verily

Allah guideth whom He will."

Verse 24:46
"Verily We have sent down revelations and explained them. Allah guideth whom He will unto a straight path."

Verse 30:29
"Nay, but those who do wrong follow their own lusts without knowledge. Who is able to guide him whom Allah hath sent astray? For such there are no helpers."

Verse 35:8
"Is he, the evil of whose deeds is made fairseeming unto him so that he deemeth it good, (other than Satan's dupe)? Allah verily sendeth whom He will astray, and guideth whom He will; so let not thy soul expire in sighings for them. Lo! Allah is Aware of what they do!"

Verse 39:23
"......... Such is Allah's guidance, wherewith He guideth whom He will. And him whom Allah sendeth astray, for him there is no guide."

Verse 39:36
"Will not Allah defend His slave? Yet they would frighten thee with those beside Him. He whom

Allah sendeth astray, for him there is no guide."

Verse 39:37
"And he whom Allah guideth, for him there can be no misleader. Is not Allah Mighty, Able to Requite (the wrong)?"

Verse 74:53
"Nay, verily. They fear not the Hereafter."

Verse 74:54
"Nay, verily. Lo! this is an Admonishment."

Verse 74:55
"So whosoever will may heed."

Verse 74:56
"And they will not heed unless Allah willeth (it). He is the fount of fear. He is the fount of Mercy."

30. During an attempt to read translation of the Qur'an by Pickthal, word to word of Arabic and English, I was struck reading verse 62 of Surah Al-Baqara. It appeared to offer a different angle to our usual concept of faith offering a question not satisfactorily answered as far as I know – are all non muslims destined to go to hell, and do we born muslims, by that stroke of luck, have a good chance of landing in paradise (of whatever level

of grace out of the said to be seven)? Some time later, on reaching verse 69 of Surah Al-Maida, I went back to 2:62 and found these identical and the subject matter critically important. Was I reading it right?! But the words were crystal clear and so the meaning! Allow me to interject that I had never formally learnt Arabic but so many of its words appeared akin to Urdu that I was mostly able to make a fair guess of the desired meaning in the English translation. However reading word to word was taking a lot of time. So, on reaching the next Surah (Al-Inam), I decided to read only the translation alongside the 'Tafaseer' available with me, for explanation and clarification of points not fully understood in the translation. As I continued to read I came across a few more verses, one or two very recently, supportive of what I had understood earlier. Being related to the matter of Faith, which again is directly related to Jihad, I decided to bring it up here. So, please, cast a careful look on the related verses:

Verse 2:62
"Lo! Those who believe (in that which is revealed unto thee, Muhammad), and those who are Jews, and Christians, and Sabaeans - whoever believeth in Allah and the Last Day and doeth right - surely their reward is with their Lord, and there shall no fear come upon them neither shall they grieve."

Verse 2:111

"And they say: None entereth paradise unless he be a Jew or a Christian. These are their own desires. Say: Bring your proof (of what ye state) if ye are truthful."

Verse 2:212

"Beautified is the life of the world for those who disbelieve; they make a jest of the believers. But those who keep their duty to Allah will be above them on the Day of Resurrection. Allah giveth without stint to whom He will."

Verse 2:213

"Mankind were one community, and Allah sent (unto them) prophets as bearers of good tidings and as warners, and revealed therewith the Scripture with the truth that it might judge between mankind concerning that wherein they differed. And only those unto whom (the Scripture) was given differed concerning it, after clear proofs had come unto them, through hatred one of another. And Allah by His Will guided those who believe unto the truth of that concerning which they differed. Allah guideth whom He will unto a straight path."

Verse 4:57

"And as for those who believe and do good works, We shall make them enter Gardens underneath which rivers flow - to dwell therein for ever; there for them are pure companions - and We shall make them enter plenteous shade."

Verse 5:69
"Lo! those who believe, and those who are Jews, and Sabaeans, and Christians - Whosoever believeth in Allah and the Last Day and doeth right - there shall no fear come upon them neither shall they grieve."

Verse 22:17
"Lo! those who believe (this revelation), and those who are Jews, and the Sabaeans and the Christians and the Magians and the idolaters - Lo! Allah will decide between them on the Day of Resurrection. Lo! Allah is Witness over all things."

Verse 39:3
"Surely pure religion is for Allah only. And those who choose protecting friends beside Him (say): We worship them only that they may bring us near unto Allah. Lo! Allah will judge between them concerning that wherein they differ. Lo! Allah guideth not him who is a liar, an ingrate."

Verse 7:170
"And as for those who make (men) keep the Scripture, and establish worship - lo! We squander not the wages of reformers."

The words and the meanings of the verses are clear:

a. The most important point is the comprehensive assurance being given to peoples of all the faiths and creeds including idolaters who profess belief in Allah and the Last Day and do right, that they will be rewarded for their right conduct and good deeds by their Lord on the Day of Resurrection; no fear and no grief for them. In other words such people will not be doomed to hell, even if not destined to go to Paradise which is promised exclusively to those who believe in the Prophet hood of Muhammad (PBUH) as the last Prophet of Al-Islam (4:57 above). Thus the matter of reward for all the others is between them and their (and our) Lord. And we, even if good Muslims, are not allowed to decide fate of peoples of other faiths as long as they are not found actively opposing cause of Al-Islam.

b. The mankind is one community and Allah sent Prophets to caution them of right and wrong on the basis of what was contained in the scriptures but they differed due to hatred one of another (2:213) and fought with one another (2:253 para 31 above) on account of the schism. Allah is well aware of all their claims and will decide between them on the Day of Resurrection (22:17). My comment is that if we read 'Muslim Ummah' in place of 'mankind' above, it may appropriately apply to us today, both internationally as well as at the national level. In the latter case extremely dangerous schism is operating with ever increasing ferocity, the state watching like a helpless identity. God will of course decide on all this on the Day of Resurrection but all of us will be explaining the part we played. I have touched on this in para 26 above quoting verse 32 of Al-Maida.

31. It is clear that the Qur'an does not approve of proselytizing through coercion. It also does not allow violence; rather it ordains peaceful preaching through persuasion and logic which should appeal to the hearts and minds of the recipients such that faith may come as a matter of free will. However the ground reality is that even the prophets did not succeed in convincing and winning over large numbers of their compatriots in support of their pronounced mission. Even a series of miracles did not work. The Prophets Daud and Suleiman were kings while Yousaf became a top state functionary. Musa succeeded through a long arduous struggle aided by miracles and "evident authority" (4:153). Case of Jesus Christ son of Mary was the latest example of open ended divine support through miracles which would have affected a worst skeptic but nothing worked. And God decided:

Surah 'Ale 'Imran

Verse 55

"(And remember) when Allah said: O Jesus! Lo! I am gathering thee and causing thee to ascend unto Me, and am cleansing thee of those who disbelieve and am setting those who follow thee above those who disbelieve until the Day of Resurrection. Then unto Me ye will (all) return, and I shall judge between you as to that wherein ye used to differ."

The only exception was Prophet Muhammad (PBUH). But perhaps not! The Qur'an is a constant miracle. It threw a challenge to produce a few lines like it; but no one picked up the gauntlet:

Surah Al-Baqarah

Verse 23

"And if ye are in doubt concerning that which We reveal unto Our slave (Muhammad), then produce a surah of the like thereof, and call your witness beside Allah if ye are truthful."

Verse 24

"And if ye do it not - and ye can never do it - then guard yourselves against the Fire prepared for disbelievers, whose fuel is of men and stones."

But today we are in a different world with super computers and the brains behind these. And we have a body called The United Nations Organization whose job it is to reconcile and pacify conflicting interests. Would they be ready to constitute a Commission of scholars, preferably religious, and linguists to accept the above challenge? Their handiwork, if they ever are able to produce one, should then be examined by another similar commission with a mingling of Jurists of that level, and give their findings. Call me naive if you like, because I mean what I say. But what about those who may think that no effort would have been made in this regard during the last millennium and a half. Okay, if Qur'an is not a miracle, job of the Prophet becomes ever more difficult. To get an idea of his effort and the extent of his success, let us have a look on what non adherent scholars and philosophers have to say about him:

French scholar, Lamartine says:

"If greatness of purpose, smallness of means, and astounding results are the three criteria of human genius, who could dare to compare any great man in modern history with Muhammad. The most famous men created arms, laws and empires only. They founded, if anything at all, no more than material powers which often crumbled away before their eyes. This man moved not only armies, legislations, empires, peoples and dynasties but millions of men in one-third of the then inhabited world; and more than that, he moved the altars, the gods, the religions, the ideas, the beliefs and souls. On the basis of a Book, every letter of which has become law, he created a spiritual nationality, which blended together people of every tongue and of every race. He has left for us as the indelible characteristic of the Muslim nationality, the hatred of the false gods and the passion for the one and immaterial God. Philosopher, orator, apostle, legislator, warrior, conqueror of ideas, restorer of rational dogmas, of a cult without images, the founder of twenty terrestrial empires and of one spiritual empire, that is Muhammad. As regards all standards by which human greatness may be measured we may well ask, is there any man greater than he is?"

(Historledela Turquie, Paris, Vol. 1, pp. 276-277 by Lamartine).

British scholar, George Bernard Shaw says:

"I have always held the religion of Muhammad in high estimation because of its wonderful vitality. It is the only religion, which appears to possess that assimilating capability to the changing phases of existence which can make itself appeal to every age. I have prophesied about the faith of Muhammad that it would be acceptable tomorrow as it is beginning to be acceptable to the Europe of today. Medieval ecclesiastics, either through ignorance or bigotry, painted Muhammadanism in the darkest colors. They were, in fact, trained to hate both the man Muhammad and his religion. To them Muhammad was anti-Christ. I have studied him, the wonderful man, and in my opinion far from being an anti-Christ he must be called a savior of Humanity. I believe that if a man like him were to assume the dictatorship of the modern world he would succeed in solving the problems in a way that would bring it the much-needed peace and happiness. Europe is beginning to be enamored of the creed of the Muhammad. In the next century it may go still further in recognizing the utility of that creed in solving its problems, and it is in this sense that you must understand my prediction."

('A collection of Writings of some of the Eminent Scholars' p. 77, by the Woking Muslims Mission, 1933 edition).

32. Let me admit I thought I had said all that I had to say on Jihad, and declared my study complete to Fatima who had been typing it, and retyping the corrected drafts. However, in the heart of my

82

hearts I felt the study should have ended with a positive outcome in the form of a line of action. Line of action obviously is that we Muslims must strive individually as well as collectively that Al-Islam prevails over all religions. We are told that there shall be no prophet after Prophet Muhammad (PBUH). However, we have the Qur'an and example of the Prophet to guide us on. We have to do our best to follow in his footsteps to be able to earn Paradise. But we have already agreed that with the exception of one – the last – very few prophets appeared to have met with any resounding success in their fairly long life times despite the miracles in their support. So then one is bound to feel too small! Let us therefore go back to the Qur'an:

Surah Al-Baqarah Verse 286

"Allah tasketh not a soul beyond its scope. For it (is only) that which it hath earned, and against it (only) that which it hath deserved. Our Lord! Condemn us not if we forget, or miss the mark! Our Lord! Lay not on us such a burden as thou didst lay on those before us! Our Lord! Impose not on us that which we have not the strength to bear! Pardon us, absolve us and have mercy on us, Thou, our Protector, and give us victory over the disbelieving folk."

Surah Al-'A`raf Verse 42

"But (as for) those who believe and do good works - We tax not any soul beyond its scope - Such are rightful owners of the Garden. They abide therein." Thus God wants us to only do our best (and He knows all). As for the Prophet, it is interesting to note how God appreciates the quality of his striving:

Surat Al-'Ahzab Verse 56

"Lo! Allah and His angels shower blessings on the Prophet. O ye who believe! Ask blessings on him and salute him with a worthy salutation."
Very remarkable! Yes! So, wondering where and when I had read this or a similar verse earlier, I started looking for it. When located, it struck me in the same way as verse 62 of Al-Baqarah (Para 32 Ibid). It came out to be verse 43 of the same Surah just about two pages earlier, but had, perhaps, been read with a longish time gap due, probably, to some very important matters covered in between these two verses. Kindly bear with me on this conjectural explanation to a factual situation. However here is it:

Surat Al-'Ahzab Verse 43

"He it is Who blesseth you, and His angels (bless you), that He may bring you forth from darkness unto light; and He is ever Merciful to the believers." Let us have a look at the Arabic text of the verses which may facilitate to draw analogy between the two:

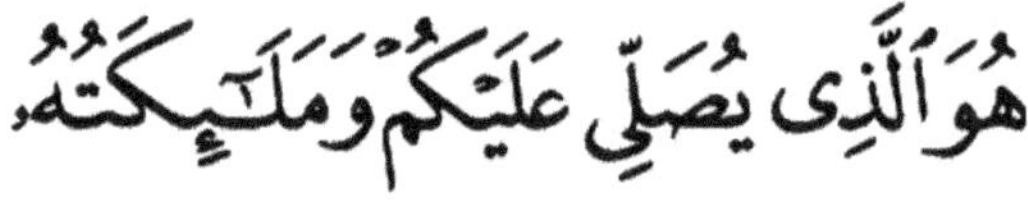

V-43

 He it is Who blesseth you, and His angels (bless you)

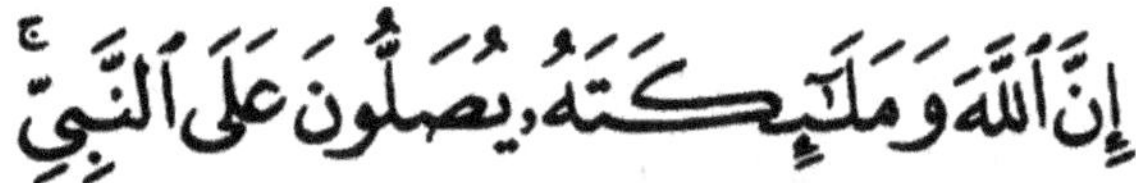

V-56

Lo! Allah and His angels shower blessings on the Prophet.

All I am implying is that the Prophet having been already blessed, anyone and everyone sincerely striving in the way of Allah, can hope to be included amongst those being blessed by Him and His angels. That is why the Prophet advised the word 'Aal' (آل) to be included in the specific prayer called 'درود' (Tafheem Ul Qur'an, Volume 4, Page 126, Note 107) invoking blessings of God for the Prophet; where ' آل ' means all those who have surrendered their will and purpose to Allah and have bartered this life for the next:

Verse 3:20
"And if they argue with thee, (O Muhammad), say: I have surrendered my purpose to Allah and (so have) those who follow me. And say unto those who have received the Scripture and those who read not: Have ye (too) surrendered? If they surrender, then truly they are rightly guided, and if they turn away, then it is thy duty only to convey the message (unto them). Allah is Seer of (His) bondmen."

Verse 4:74
"Let those fight in the way of Allah who sell the life of this world for the other. Whoso fighteth in the way of Allah, be he slain or be he victorious, on him We shall bestow a vast reward."

33. Having gone through what Qur'an says on Jihad, and how the Prophet acted on the God's Ordinances in this regard, our study can be more fruitful if related to the objective contemporary conditions to see what we need to do here. And this can clearly be seen as a most challenging proposition. A lot of highly motivated and committed people would have striven at individual as well as at collective level, even at the cost of their lives, that Al-Islam may again prevail over all religions. I am here talking in terms of the history of the last half

millennium when Islam was no more the dominant faith. The Muslim world continued to lose its religious moorings, and in the last one century or so the antagonist powers have tried hard to turn them into a pariah entity. It is pointless blaming others for the sad state of affairs the Muslim world finds itself in. The inimical forces (as one group) are too strong while we are too divided to be able to make a dent. An effort was made in 1974 but, soon enough, all the three characters behind it were eliminated (as would all concerned recollect). Ever since the situation has gone from bad to worse, and may appear irredeemable to the more discernable minds. Fate of Al-Qaida is before us. For all their commitment they stand dispersed. And if the narrative of 9/11 is true, then, ironically, their achievement was to have been cause of the destruction of Iraq and the quasi occupation of that country now being torn apart through sectarian strife. Al-Qaida may also be considered, by default, responsible for the reelection of Mr. George Bush to attack Afghanistan with dubious intentions. The Taliban of Afghanistan were not a clandestine organization. They were a legitimate government of a sovereign country who refused to hand over a fugitive Muslim fighter purely on the suspicion of having acted against the US who, as the self styled sponsor of the so called 'New World Order', and, unprecedentedly undeterred by any one, launched their biggest offensive war after the Vietnam, dispersed government of a sovereign state, and installed a puppet regime there. However, an unprecedented resilient guerilla war by the Taliban has forced the Western world (NATO and ISAF) to negotiate for peace. By any standards of morality and international law, a totally unjustified war was launched by the US, later joined up by other Western countries quite possibly with their eyes on the spoils of war – huge reserves of natural resources of Central Asia – which is yet making them drag their feet. Anyway it is clear that the Taliban fought back in self defence in the spirit of 'fighting in the cause of Allah' to oust the 'infidel' invaders who, intoxicated by the, so to say, unchallengeable war machine at their disposal, committed open aggression against a recognized sovereign country, on flimsy grounds. This is 'JIHAD'.

34.   But then what is Tehrik-e-Taliban Pakistan (TTP) fighting for? They want Sharia! Is there any country in the world whose constitution lays down that Sovereignty belongs to Almighty Allah; that there shall be no law against the provisions of Qur'an and Sunnah. It lays down that a non muslim cannot be Head of the state or the government, and that interest based economy is un-Islamic (which amounts to fighting against the whole world).

Stand of the TTP and scores of its affiliates, does not appear tenable. Their actions are causing untold misery (in the mildest words) to thousands of innocent people besides bringing bad name to the country and the Muslim 'Ummah'. Islam is being termed synonymous with terrorism. A self righteous attitude is not fair. Is there any sanction to kill your fellow Muslim brothers indiscriminately through IED's or through suicide bombers? Is there sanction to kill innocent non-muslims who were not lucky enough to be born Muslims and did not happen to learn of the spirit of Islam? Is there not a strict edict that killing of a single person other than for manslaughter or corruption in the earth is like killing of all mankind? There can be so many such genuine or rhetorical questions. Best course would be we go back to Qur'an. Are there any edicts different in content to what has been discussed in this study earlier? And in case of varying interpretation, can we sit down to discuss these threadbare with a sincere intention to end the schism? If finally we don't agree, you can walk away, both sides then being answerable to the 'All Knowing'. Or, have you a different agenda which would not allow an informed discourse! In that case, the Government of Pakistan has to come up with a balanced but clear counter terrorism policy to restore writ of the state at all cost, and soon enough.

35. In the nearly two dozen verses quoted in paras
     30 and 32 above, we noticed God's Decree
     that granting faith and guidance is solely His
     prerogative. The purpose would be that none of
     the mankind is allowed to arrogate to himself the
     authority to decide about the faith of the others.
     But reading out of context against the spirit of
     the above quoted verses, a non serious person can
     consider himself absolved of any responsibility
     in this regard and act as would please him. We
     could have discussed this just after para 29 on the
     subject of faith but I decided to bring it up at the
     end of this study because matter of belief/faith is
     critically important as it forms the rock bottom for
     our behavior towards life. God has endowed the
     human kind with the all important guide termed
     'conscience' which distinguishes them from other
     living beings. It enables us to decide between right
     and wrong entitling us to the exercise of free will
     and freedom of action though on a limited scale;
     yet that is where the problem starts. A successful
     self sufficient person has the tendency to become
     proud and arrogant overlooking the role of God in
     all his affairs. Thus the matter of faith may start
     appearing superfluous to him; denying and defying
     becomes his habit or second nature. Here we are
     addressing mainly such 'lucky' persons as well
     as the other non serious ones mentioned earlier.
     God repeatedly emphasizes that we should ponder

and reflect on all the natural phenomena around us including our own personal beings. He further ordains that we pay heed and not be neglectful towards His teachings, and terms people having an opposite attitude being like deaf, dumb and blind, equating such people to cattle. There is yet another category of people who want clear cut and visible proofs in support of the revealed matters. They want angels to come to them, they want to see God, and want the dead to speak. They think this is clever, and are proud of such machinations. Let us see how the Qur'an admonishes all these categories of people:

Surah Al-Baqarah (2)

Verse 6
"As for the Disbelievers, Whether thou warn them or thou warn them not it is all one for them; they believe not."

Verse 7
"Allah hath sealed their hearing and their hearts, and on their eyes there is a covering. Theirs will be an awful doom."

Verse 18
"Deaf, dumb and blind; and they return not."

Surah Al-'An`am (6)

Verse 39

"Those who deny Our revelations are deaf and dumb in darkness. Whom Allah will sendeth astray, and whom He will He placeth on a straight path."

Verse 111

"And though We should send down the angels unto them, and the dead should speak unto them, and We should gather against them all things in array, they would not believe unless Allah so willed. Howbeit, most of them are ignorant."

Verse 126

"This is the path of thy Lord, a straight path. We have detailed Our revelations for a people who take heed."

Surah Al-'A`raf (7)

Verse 179

"Already have We urged unto hell many of the jinn and humankind, having hearts wherewith they understand not, and having eyes wherewith they see not, and having ears wherewith they hear not. These are as the cattle - nay, but they are worse! These are the neglectful."

Surah Al-'Anfal (8)

Verse 22

"Lo! the worst of beasts in Allah's sight are the deaf, the dumb, who have no sense."

Verse 55

"Lo! the worst of beasts in Allah's sight are the ungrateful who will not believe."

Surah Al-Furqan (25)

Verse 21

"And those who look not for a meeting with Us say: Why are angels not sent down unto us and (Why) do we not see our Lord! Assuredly they think too highly of themselves and are scornful with great pride."

Surah Fatir (35)

Verse 28

"..................... The erudite among His bondmen fear Allah alone. Lo! Allah is Mighty, Forgiving."

Surah Az-Zumar (39)

Verse 9
"Is he who payeth adoration in the watches of the night, prostrate and standing, bewaring of the Hereafter and hoping for the mercy of his Lord, (to be accounted equal with a disbeliever)? Say (unto them, O Muhammad): Are those who know equal with those who know not? But only men of understanding will pay heed.

Surah Al-Jathiyah (45)

Verse 13
"And hath made of service unto you whatsoever is in the heavens and whatsoever is in the earth; it is all from Him. Lo! herein verily are portents for a people who reflect."

Surah Al-Mujadila (58)

Verse 11
".................... Allah will exalt those who believe among you, and those who have knowledge, to high ranks. Allah is Informed of what ye do."

" I shall pass through this world but once.
Any good that I can do or any help that I can give
to my fellow beings let me do it now, for I shall not
pass this way again."
-Anonymous

A quote I cannot finish reading without eyes getting wet, sometimes overflowing, probably on account of regret for not having been able to make it a guiding principle in life.

Brig. (R) Najeeb Ullah Khan
Lahore: October 01, 2013

Notes

Notes